DRAWING YOUR LIFE

Learning to See, Record and Appreciate Life's Small Joys

Michael Nobbs

A Perigee Book

A PERIGEE BOOK
Published by the Penguin Group
Penguin Group (USA) Inc.
375 Hudson Street, New York, New York 10014, USA

Penguin Group (Canada), 90 Eglinton Avenue East, Suite 700, Toronto, Ontario M4P 2Y3,
Canada (a division of Pearson Penguin Canada Inc.) • Penguin Books Ltd., 80 Strand,
London WC2R 0RL, England • Penguin Ireland, 25 St. Stephen's Green, Dublin 2, Ireland
(a division of Penguin Books Ltd.) • Penguin Group (Australia), 707 Collins Street, Melbourne,
Victoria 3008, Australia (a division of Pearson Australia Group Pty Ltd.) • Penguin Books India
Pvt. Ltd., 11 Community Centre, Panchsheel Park, New Delhi—110 017, India •
Penguin Group (NZ), 67 Apollo Drive, Rosedale, Auckland 0632, New Zealand (a division
of Pearson New Zealand Ltd.) • Penguin Books (South Africa), Rosebank Office Park,
181 Jan Smuts Avenue, Parktown North 2193, South Africa • Penguin China,
B7 Jiaming Center, 27 East Third Ring Road North, Chaoyang District, Beijing 100020, China

Penguin Books Ltd., Registered Offices: 80 Strand, London WC2R 0RL, England

DRAWING YOUR LIFE

First edition: March 2013

ISBN: 978-0-399-16113-1

PRINTED IN THE UNITED STATES OF AMERICA

10 9 8 7 6 5 4 3 2 1

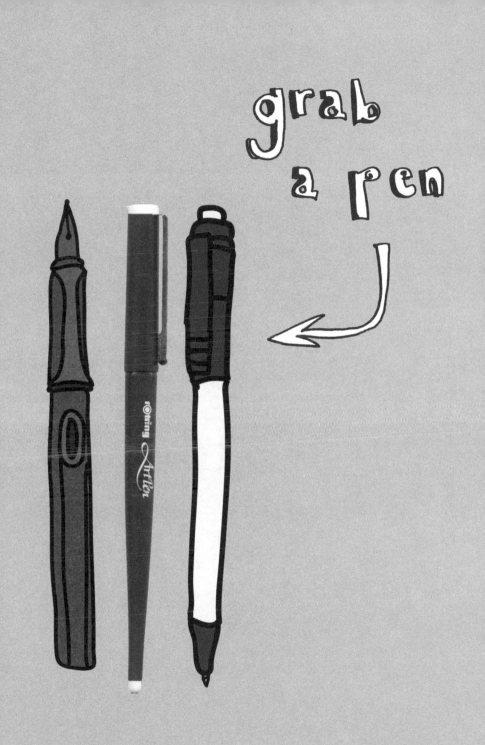

...and begin
a lifelong

journey

DRAW THE FIRST THING

Make a start
and draw
for just two
minutes!

Don't worry what your drawing looks like.
Just put pen to paper!

THAT CATCHES YOUR EYE!

BRIEF

Introduction

→

I'm Michael Nobbs, a full-time artist, blogger and tea drinker (not necessarily in that order).

I live in Britain (hence all the tea I drink!) and I've been drawing my life for quite a few years now.

Back at the end of the 1990s I was diagnosed with **ME/CFS.*** Learning to draw was a huge help in coming to terms with my health challenges and showed me how to live (and enjoy!) my life in a new way.

Some people have photo albums, I have drawings. I've drawn the people I've loved, the places I've been, the world around me (and an awful lot of cups of tea!).

I hope this book will encourage you to draw **YOUR LIFE** and perhaps show you a way you can enjoy each day just a little bit more.

*Myalgic Encephalomyelitis/Chronic Fatigue Syndrome is an illness that means I'm a lot like an old rechargeable battery that can't hold much of a charge. Each day I have a limited amount of useful energy to work with and do my best to make each ounce count!

Drink tea, eat biscuits and do one small creative thing every day (and sometimes draw your teapot)

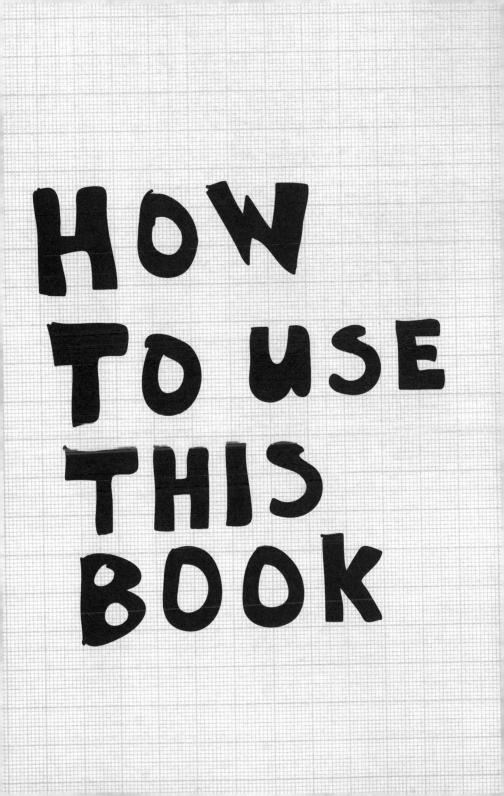

HOW TO USE THIS BOOK

It's never too late to start to draw and remember (even though you might not think so) **EVERYBODY** can draw!

1. Follow the instructions
(or make up your own).

2. Draw anywhere.*

3. Rip out pages.

4. Stick in new pages.

5. Make lots of
"mistakes."

6. Have fun!

1. Carry this book (or a small sketchbook) everywhere.

2. Keep a favorite pen in your pocket/bag.

3. Get them both out regularly.

4. Draw!

Create a portable studio

(so you can draw anytime/anywhere)

Instructions

REMEMBER: By working little and often it is possible to build a substantial body of work—and even a creative career!

YOUR PORTABLE STUDIO

If you're limited in terms of time or energy, then creating a portable studio (and always having it with you) is the perfect way of making sure that you can always make the best use of your resources.

At its simplest a portable studio can be just a small sketchbook and pen that you slip in your pocket or bag whenever you leave the house.

Better still, set aside a dedicated bag to be your portable studio. Spend some time thinking about the tools you need to be able to work anywhere and gather them together in your bag.

Once you have your portable studio, you'll never need to waste time (and energy) looking for your tools; they'll always be in one place. Now you'll be able to set to work instantly, making use of even the smallest amounts of time to do a little creative work.

Portable Studio Checklist

(Add the tools _you_ need)

- [ ] **Pen**

- [ ] **Sketchbook**

- [ ] _____

- [ ] _____

- [ ] _____

- [ ] _____

- [ ] _____

Be
Curious!

READ INSPIRING BOOKS

Reading List

- [ ] **The Artist's Way**
  by Julia Cameron

- [ ] **The Zen of Seeing**
  by Frederick Franck

- [ ] **How to Be an Explorer of the World**
  by Keri Smith

- [ ] **Drawing on the Right Side of the Brain**
  by Betty Edwards

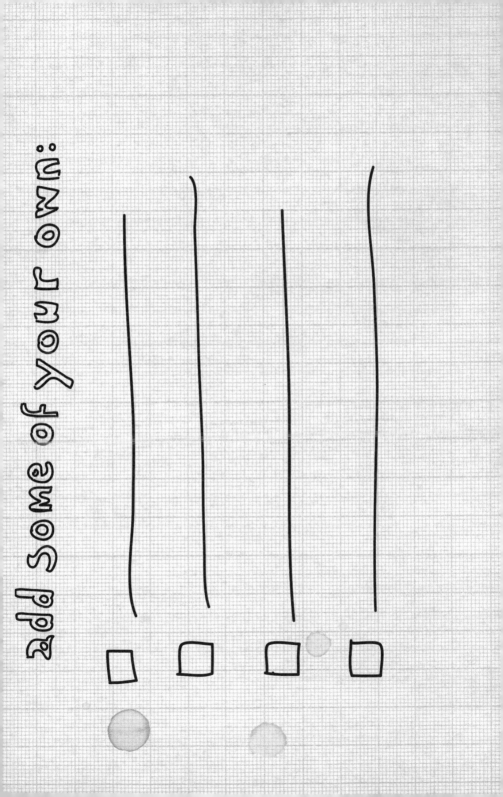

add some of your own:

If you know my work, you probably know that I love to draw the everyday and ordinary. If you're going to draw your own life, you'll probably have to embrace doing the same.

Whilst I think everyone's life is unique and full of interest, that uniqueness is often made up of the mundane: the endless cups of tea you drink, the food you eat, the dishes you wash, the things in your bathroom, the pile of books by your bed. They all go together to make up the richness that is your life.

By all means draw the out-of-the-ordinary too (the birthdays you celebrate, the places you go on holiday, a visit to an art gallery), but don't wait for the extraordinary to happen.

Draw the everyday and ordinary.

Start today with what's in front of you. Draw any object, a teacup perhaps, and then find another and another and draw those too.

Make a
series of
drawings of
similar things.

I drew brushes.
**WHAT WILL
YOU DRAW?**

YOUR
DRAWING
MISSIONS

Breakfast is my favorite meal of the day—and the perfect time to start your drawing life.

Start your new drawing adventure by treating yourself to breakfast in a cafe.

I love to meet friends for breakfast (and maybe a little drawing)

Draw your knife and for your breakfast

(or you could copy mine)

fork while you wait
to arrive ...

DRaw your condiments

Draw your breakfast
(or your empty plate!)

Drawing is about learning to see (really see!) the world around you.

Try this:

Turn the page and draw something that's in front of you right now, but draw it without looking at the paper. Follow the outline of the object you're looking at and let your pen just wander across the paper.

This can be a scary exercise to try. Make it easier by having a mug of tea or coffee at your side for company and comfort.

You have absolute permission to make the worst drawing ever here. It will be absolutely perfect just as it is.

Draw something here without looking at the page

Draw something here without looking at the page

I regularly stop during the day for a pot of tea to pause and reflect on how my day is going. Why not take your own pause today and draw your tea or coffee cup.

Tea breaks are even better if there's a slice of cake involved!

Treat yourself to

DRAW IT!

a slice of cake

My art is that of living. Each second, each breath is a work which is inscribed nowhere.

—Marcel Duchamp

There's no need to change your life in order to start to draw it. It is perfect and unique and interesting just as it is.

Embrace your life just as it is.

That boiled egg you ate for breakfast is the art. That cup of tea you drank with a slice of cake is the art. That trip you took to the shops is the art. The contents of your bathroom shelf is the art.

Embrace it all. Record it all.

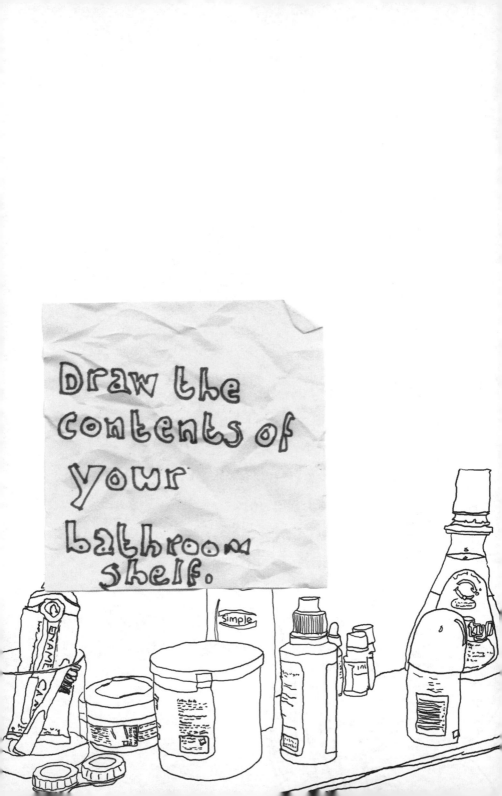

1. Run a bath.
2. Add bubbles.
3. Get in.
4. Soak.
5. Draw!

Don't worry about getting this book wet.
It will only add character to your drawing...

SET A TIMER AND DRAW

FOR TWENTY MINUTES

Take a break and then turn the page →

Do the previous page first

DRAW FOR FIFTEEN MINUTES MORE

To escape
Criticism –
do nothing,
say nothing,
~~do~~ be nothing.

—Elbert
Hubbard

Don't be scared! Draw something
you think you can't draw!

Pick something that adds joy to your day...

DRAW IT!

DRAW YOUR LAUNDRY HANGING ON THE LINE

The smell of line-dried laundry is definitely one of life's joys...

Draw somewhere you just happen to be.

Draw in a car, bus, train or plane.

COLOU
PENC

12

pencils

Treat yourself to some new colored pens,
pencils or crayons (or all three!)

Try them out here

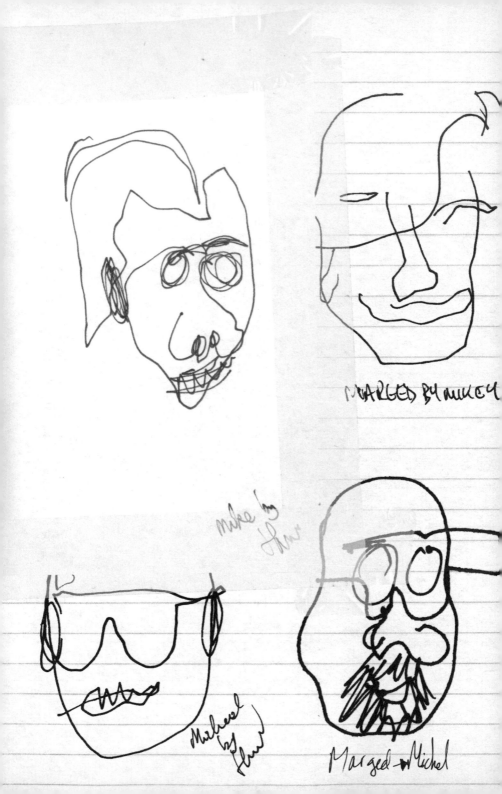

MARGED BY MIKEY

mike by Shan

Michael by Shan

Marged Michel

Hold a PORTRAIT PARTY

Miguel by Neil.

Earlier in the book I asked you to make a drawing without looking at the paper. Now I'm going to ask you to invite some friends round and draw portaits of each other without looking at the paper.

Make a party out of the event. Tell everyone it isn't important what the drawings look like. What's important is that you all have fun and that you practice looking, really looking, at what you're drawing (rather than looking at the drawing!)

When we first start to draw we have a tendency to draw what we "think" we see, rather than what we're actually looking at. We also often worry about what our drawing looks like and that can make us too nervous to actually put pen to paper.

Tell your friends to hold their pens very lightly and then just let the pen flow gently over the paper as they look closely at the person they're drawing.

MICHAEL BY
MIKEY

Draw portraits of your friends without looking at the paper!

Give all your friends pages from a sketchbook and ask them to draw each other.

1. Draw on any scraps of paper you can find.

2. Glue, tape or clip your drawings here.

Did you know this napkin is made from 100% recycled

Draw something on this napkin (then find your own napkin and draw someting else)

Make <u>lots</u> of
bad drawings
(and lern not
to care!)

(mistakes add character)

(or draw while you're talking on the phone

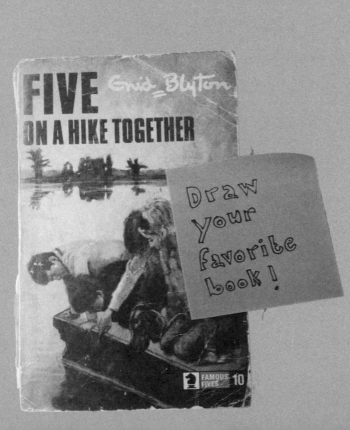

FIVE
ON A HIKE TOGETHER

Enid Blyton

FAMOUS FIVES 10

Draw your favorite book!

Go for a walk and draw three things that you see

1.

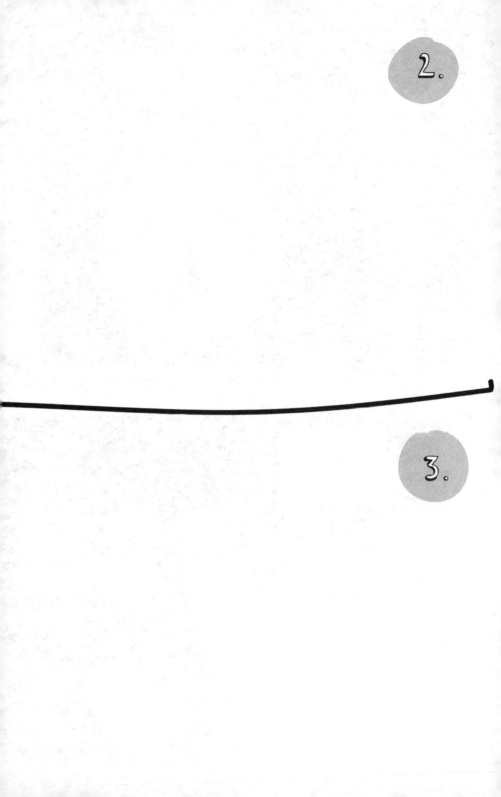

OPEN A CUPBOARD AT RANDOM
AND DRAW THE CONTENTS

SLOW DOWN

(and start to REALLY see the world!)

Drawing helps us slow down, live in the moment and truly see the world around us. As one of my drawing heroes **Frederick Franck** says, "Seeing/drawing is a way of contemplation by which all things are made new, by which the world is freshly experienced at each moment."

TRY THIS:

Choose an object that you see in your environment every day. Spend five minutes truly looking at it. Follow its contours, examine the shapes that make it up, drink in its colors. Now, pick up your pen and slowly, VERY slowly, draw what you have been looking at.

BE PREPARED FOR YOUR LIFE TO CHANGE!

Don't be surprised if as the more you slow down and start to see the world through the eyes of someone who draws that you suddenly have the urge to enjoy other things in life at a slower pace! You might find you want to cook from scratch, make your coffee in a pot, go for a stroll, sit on a park bench or even take an afternoon nap.

Make a pot of fresh coffee and sit and slowly enjoy it.

Draw your coffeepot

Give up watching one TV show and draw instead
(you could even draw your TV)

Draw your favorite TV show!

Draw while
you're waiting
for something
to happen...

MICRO-DRAWING: Make use of those tiny spare moments of time in your day, perhaps when you're in a line, waiting for an appointment or just while your kettle boils!

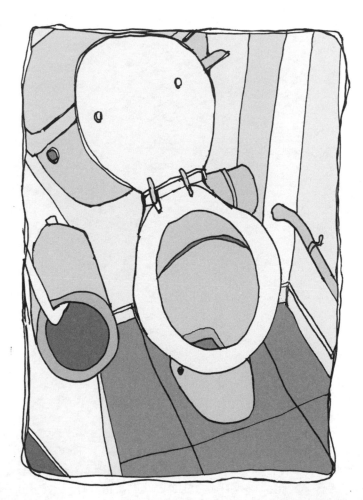

Draw while you're sitting on the toilet!

1. Find an old photo of yourself.

2. Draw it.

David Hockney
used to make a
self-portrait in
the mirror on his
birthday each year.

Draw yourself in the mirror

1. Find an old photo of someone from your family.
2. Draw it.
3. Cut it out (or photocopy it) and put it in a frame.

Draw a mother (yours or someone else's)

Draw a father (yours or someone else's)

Start to make a drawn photo album of the people you love

Drawing in public can be a scary step to take, but there are so many wonderful places to visit and things to record that it's well worth taking that step...

DRAWING
IN
PUBLIC

Grab your portable studio* and head out for a drawing adventure...

instructions for making your portable studio are at the beginning of the book

Drawing in public can be daunting at first. Start gently. Instead of drawing the people, places and things you see, start by drawing something familar that you have with yo

Go to a cafe and draw the tools in your portable studio...

DRAW IN A PUBLIC PLACE

Record the date, time and place of your drawings

Go somewhere specifically to draw — a museum, a gallery, a library, a bookshop, a cafe...

Tate Modern in London is my favorite gallery, full of wonderful drawing opportunities (and a great cafe!)

DRAW A STRANGER

1. Meet some friends.
2. Give them all paper and a pen.
3. Draw together.
4. Stick your drawings here.
CITY
NIGHT

1. Take photos of things you'd like to draw while you're out and about but are too nervous/haven't time to draw.

2. Draw from the photos when you get home.

Draw while you listen to the radio

Draw your pet
(if you haven't got a pet, draw a friend's)

Why not draw a friend's pet, put it in a frame and give it to them as a gift?

Framing your work helps you value it.

WORK WITHIN YOUR LIMITS

All of us, even the fittest and healthiest, have limits. If w
learn to accept and work within our own limits (and stop
comparing ourselves to others) we will thrive and begin to
produce work that is uniquely our own.

Feeling under the weather?
Just make a very small drawing

Draw the contents of your bag, backpack or pocket

STAND UP
AND DRAW
SOMETHING

(apparently, standing while we work has health benefits, though
I'm rather a fan of doing plenty of sitting and relaxing too)

Draw your favorite food

Draw your least favorite food

When I was very ill back at the end of the 1990s, I signed up for a weekly drawing class. I couldn't manage to attend every class but went along whenever I could. I made new friends (and lots of bad drawings!) and slowly started to see the world through new eyes.

SIGN UP FOR A

DRAWING CLASS

Treat yourself to something you love to do but seldom take the time for.

Draw the experience.

My choice would be go out for a very British afternoon tea and to draw the sandwiches! What will you do?

Draw something unusual that you've seen in a catalog, shop or online store...

Draw with your non-dominant hand...

A great way to practice making "bad" drawings and not to care

Collect together five unusual things that you own

DRAW THEM!

Go on, you can do it!

BAKE A CAKE
(and draw the ingredients)

1. Sort out some things you no longer want.

2. Draw them before you throw them away/recycle/ give to charity.

1. Always keep some
pens or pencils within
easy reach.

2. Reach for them
regularly!

GRAB A PEN RIGHT NOW AND DRAW
ANYTHING YOU WANT

DRAW YOUR
FAVORITE PEN

(using your second favorite pen)

Collect together your

five favorite things

Draw them

DRAW YOUR HAND

DRAW YOUR OTHER HAND
(you might find this a little harder!)

DRAW YOUR SHOES

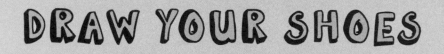

1. TAKE OFF YOUR SHOES.

2. DRAW YOUR FEET.

DRAW YOUR K-YS

Draw from memory

Think of something that made you smile. Draw it!

DRAW FROM IMAGINATION

When we were children we drew from our imaginations all the time. It was fun!

Recapture that feeling.

DRAW YOUR DINNER

Draw your dirty dishes

(or just your washing-up liquid bottle)

Draw your clean dishes

Sit quietly and think about something that has added a little joy to your day today. Write about it below—you could draw a picture too!

SET YOUR ALARM TEN MINUTES EARLIER FOR TOMORROW

DRAW THE LAST THING YOU SEE BEFORE YOU GO TO SLEEP

CONTINUING YOUR DRAWING ADVENTURE

(one step at a time!)

GOOD MORNING!

DRAW THE FIRST THING YOU SEE

Start a list of things you'd like to draw (keep adding to it)...

1.
2.
3.
4.
5.
6.
7.
8.
9.
10.
11.
12.
13.
14.
15.
16.
17.
18.
19.
20.

21.
22.
23.
24.
25.
26.
27.
28.
29.
30.
31.
32.
33.
34.
35.
36.
37.
38.
39.
40.
41.
42.
43.

1. Buy or make a (slim) sketchbook.

2. Set a date to fill it by.

3. Clip, tape or stick it here.

Some websites to visit:
www.kerismith.com
www.dannygregory.com
www.moonlightchronicles.com

Drink tea
and eat
biscuits!

Read lots of great books about
art and look at some wonderful
websites. Go to galleries. Watch
art programs on TV. In short,
immerse yourself and discover
what you love.

I made this
book one page
at a time...

What will
you do one
step at a
time?

IDEA: fill a sketchbook with one drawing a day

Acknowlegdments

This book is for Stella Margaret Nobbs who taught me how to make a lovely cup of tea. You're very missed.

I tend to move rather slowly and manage most of what I do because of the love and support of those around me.

Thank you to George Jones for always making life easier. Michael Rose and Huw Hughes for the breakfasts and pep talks, Neil Holland and Miguel Ortuño Sánchez for the sofa (and tequila), Janet Thomas for all her encouragement, Hilaire Wood and Jane MacNamee for weekly elevenses, Mary Gorden for all the cheering post, the members of Aberystwyth Writing Group for being wonderful cheerleaders and John Duff at Perigee Books for asking me to make this book and for his patience while I did.

Finally, a special and very heartfelt thanks to all the members at SustainablyCreative.com for making everything possible.

Michael Nobbs is a British artist. He currently lives on the west coast of Wales where he drinks lots of tea and takes daily naps. He is a great believer in taking small, sustainable steps on a regular basis in order to reach our goals.

Michael writes and teaches about living a sustainably creative life over on his website, SustainablyCreative.com

Find Michael online:
www.sustainablycreative.com
twitter.com/michaelnobbs
facebook.com/michaelnobbs

Have a lovely day (drink tea and make one small drawing)